SOMEONE I LOVE, LOVES SOMEONE ELSE

Book 3

By Matt Stakes

(A true story with some names changed)

Published by: **Stakes Press**

ISBN: 979-8-9939409-7-7

SOMEONE I LOVE, LOVES SOMEONE ELSE

Book 3
This is Matt's story

After some time of prayer and fasting, I gained the courage to slide into her DMs. A DM is a direct message on a social media platform. The platform we used back then was Twitter. Before sending her a message, I had been kinda stalking her page, retweeting (reposting) her posts, placing emojis in the comments, etc. This was my way of staying in her line of sight. I was preparing her for what was about to take place. I was preparing the way! And to my surprise, she was responding.

She started commenting back, reposting my tweets, and engaging in the online banter. It was surprising since we hadn't spoken in over a year at that point.

We were friends, from a distance. For 10 years, we were friends from a distance.

From what I knew from watching her socials, she had her baby, and they were doing well. If you read book two, you remember the black friday shopping story where we connected briefly to catch up. She was preggo at that time and it was beautiful to see that the baby that people thought was mine, had arrived. Read the book. Smile! Anyway, I didn't see any man on Shannon's socials, so I assumed she was single.

After my 21-day consecration time ended, I prayed to God for the courage to approach. Then I asked her out in the DMs. Yep, I sent the dm. It was probably very corny. I don't remember how I bridged the one-year gap. But after the pleasantries and 'how are you's, I said, I'd like to take you to lunch.

I'm not sure exactly how she responded, but I do remember the yes! The way she told me, she was surprised to hear from me, and thought I was suffering from a life-threatening illness and needed to talk to someone. But that wasn't the case at all. She didn't know I was about to drop the bomb of all bombs on her heart. I was about to come with the pressure. I was about to lay it all on the line. And I had no idea how she would take it.

After a few days, we met at Baker's Crust, a very quaint sandwich shop nearby. She arrived in jeans and a black embroidered vest. I was mesmerized. She always had that effect on me. Well, after getting myself together, we sat down to talk and eat.

It honestly took a minute to realize that this was real. She was actually in front of me. I was about to be the most vulnerable I'd ever been. I put fear of rejection aside and just said, "Shannon, I still love you, and I wanna try again."

As the words rolled out, I knew there was no turning back. Just like toothpaste from a tube - the words were out there and I couldn't take them back. And I didn't want to. At that moment, time stood still. She looked at me, puzzled, one eyebrow raised. Then she said, "What? I thought you had some bad news and needed someone to confide in." Then she gathered herself, contemplating. She was shaken. She didn't expect me to come with this confession. But here we were, sitting at the table, looking directly into each other's souls.

Everything from there was honestly a blur. But she gave me enough to know we were going to try. That's all I needed. At that point, we said our goodbyes, and I left the restaurant with great expectation.

According to Shannon, she immediately called her grandmother to give her the tea and ask for her input. Shannon was hesitant to try again after so much had changed in both our lives. Our careers had changed, we were both in our 30s, and we'd both been in love with other people. The last time we dated was 10 years ago, in college. It definitely felt like we'd have to get to know each other all over again.

But Grandma Lolo was hopeful. She was on my side. She told Shannon to give love a chance. She told her to open her heart. She reminded her that I was a good man. Thank you, Grandma Loretta - I love you and miss you! RIH.

Shannon decided to take GMA's advice, and we started seeing each other outside of church. Before anything, she came to me and said - 'Just so you know, I don't want a boyfriend, I want a husband.' My heart jumped, and I agreed. I told her that we were on the same page.

After that, our hangouts began. We did fun stuff like grabbing a bite to eat, watching movies, and going for walks. And every now and then, she'd cook for me. Wow, I didn't know she was such a good cook. I digress.

After about one month, I asked her to officially be my girlfriend. She said yes, and we became exclusive. I remember inviting her to see my condo for the first time. I made her dinner and dessert. Everything was going according to plan.

Even though we were 'off the market' and officially courting, we hadn't really told anyone. Our families and close friends knew. That was about it. We started doing more family activities and getting more intertwined in each other's lives.

It was time to go deeper. I noticed that Shannon was really good with money, and I was not that interested. I liked making and spending money, but budgeting wasn't my thing. So I asked her to help me with my budget. She was so excited. I brought her a shoe box with all my personal business - pay stubs, w2's, bank statements, bills, etc., and I said, " Please help me. I made decent money and had very little debt, but I wanted to have a system for my finances. Within a couple of days, she sent me a spreadsheet with all my numbers on it. It was a budget. Everything was balanced, and I even had money for savings and entertainment. I was impressed. That was just the beginning of how we started to bring out our lives together.

As much as I was applying pressure to Shannon, she was applying pressure to me. One day, I was minding my own business, and I received a text message with a picture of a beautiful diamond ring. The caption read, "This is what I want, 1 karat, round."

She always makes sure that I don't have to read her mind.

Things were progressing. The next step was to sign up for a pre-marital class. We were lucky enough to get a one-on-one class, which made it more intimate and tailor-made for us. The class was great! We discussed all the hot-button topics, and the counselor recommended a few books for us to read. Since we love books, this was great for us - homework time.

A couple of months passed, and I was ready to propose. I had the ring - exactly what she wanted - 1 karat, round, and I had the plan. So, I invited her to go on a date to the Norfolk Botanical Gardens. It was a beautiful spring day. We took the tram around the gardens, reminiscing about our very first date, over a decade ago. Our first date was in this very location - the Norfolk Botanical Gardens.

The time had come, and we reached our destination. We got off the tram and walked over to a small gazebo in the herb garden section. The funny thing is, the first time I proposed to her was in a gazebo in Hampton, Virginia. I guess we like gazebos. Anyway, there we were in the moment. It happened so fast. As soon as she entered the gazebo, I dropped to my knee and said, “Will you marry me?”

She looked so surprised, and of course, she said yes - again! We hugged, kissed, and soaked in the moment. It was a wonderful day. I couldn’t believe we were engaged for a second time. This was unreal, that God would allow us to enter each other's lives again in such a significant way. And this time felt different.

It's one thing to love each other. But another thing to be ready to commit at the same time. It's a miracle, really. The joining of two hearts requires alignment, timing, and a willingness to try. Our Baker's Crust date was in January 2010, and I proposed in April 2010.

We were engaged, excited, and off to the races! It was time for our final pre-marital class. In that class, we let the counselor know that we planned to marry in July, which was three months away. We wanted to do a small wedding with family and close friends.

Our counselor was like, "Yeah, NO." He gently suggested that we wait, giving ourselves time to plan and get things in order. We were so excited to tie the knot that this advice really took the wind out of our sails. But we decided to listen. He also asked that we consider having a larger-scale wedding so that more people could share in our big day. I was hesitant, but we once again took his advice. And of course, our parents and Shannon's Grandma agreed with him. Smile!

After considering all the advice we'd received, we decided to get married on September 4, 2010. All the stakeholders were in agreement. Stakeholders are people who invested in our wedding and our future. We were at peace with this decision. No doubts. Everything was lining up. All minds were clear. And we were excited. We made the big social media announcement and sent out the save-the-date cards.

The rest is history! I'm sure I left out a ton of details in this story. Shannon may have to fill in the gaps later. She always says that I leave out details when I tell a story. But the moral of the story is, we had to push away the fear. We did not give up on love. We created the love story that we wanted. Your story will not look like ours or anyone else's - it will be unique to you and that special person. Do what only you can do and allow God to do what only he can do. We pray that you get the love your heart desires in due time.

Other books by Stakes Press:

Someone I Love, Loves Someone Else,
Book 1 & 2 Combo (paperback)
By Shannon Stakes

The Marriage Bed (paperback)
By Shannon Stakes

Write Now! (paperback)
By Shannon Stakes

ENCOURAGEMENT
FOR CHRISTIAN
WRITERS

SHANNON STAKES

www.ingramcontent.com/pod-product-compliance
Lightning Source LLC
LaVergne TN
LVHW090543110826
845146LV00003B/1243

* 9 7 9 8 9 9 3 9 4 0 9 7 7 *